Devotions to St Thomas Becket

Devotions to
St Thomas Becket

John S. Hogan

Gracewing

First published in 2018 by
Gracewing
2 Southern Avenue
Leominster
Herefordshire HR6 0QF
United Kingdom
www.gracewing.co.uk

No part of this publication may be reproduced, stored in a retrieval system, or transmitted in any form or by any means, electronic, mechanical, photocopying, recording or otherwise, without the written permission of the publisher.

The rights of John S. Hogan to be identified as the author of this work have been asserted in accordance with the Copyright, Designs and Patents Act 1988.

© 2018 John S. Hogan

ISBN 978 085244 914 1

Typeset by Gracewing

Cover design by Bernardita Peña Hurtado

CONTENTS

Introduction..ix

A Brief Life of St Thomas Becket...........................1

Christmas Novena to St Thomas Becket............13

The Festal Invocations...31

Various Prayers to St Thomas...............................35

    Pilgrim Prayer to St Thomas Becket......................35

    Memorare to St Thomas Becket..............................37

    Novena for the Grace of Conversion......................39

    Prayer of the Sick to St Thomas Becket................41

    Litany for the Sick...43

    Prayer for Miracles..45

    Prayer to St Thomas for Chastity...........................46

    Prayer for Bishops...48

    Prayer for Priests...49

    Prayer for Courage..51

    Eucharistic Prayer to St Thomas............................52

    Prayer in a Time of Need..54

    Prayer for the Persecuted.......................................55

    Prayer for the Conversion of Souls........................56

    Litany of St Thomas Becket...................................57

The Seven Stations of St Thomas of Canterbury..........61

A Pilgrimage to Canterbury..........61

I St Dunstan's Church..........62

II The Pilgrim Walk..........66

III Canterbury Cathedral: Cloister..........70

IV Canterbury Cathedral: "The Martyrdom"..........75

V Canterbury Cathedral: The Crypt..........80

VI Canterbury Cathedral: The Site of the Tomb..........85

VII Parish Church of St Thomas of Canterbury: Martyrs' Chapel..........91

ACKNOWLEDGEMENTS

Scripture excerpts are taken from *The CTS Catholic Bible*, copyright © 2009 by The Incorporated Catholic Truth Society. Reprinted with permission.

Illustrations: A series of drawings based on images from medieval manuscripts, by a monk of Silverstream Priory, Stamullen, Co. Meath, Ireland. Reproduced with permission.

Introduction

DURING THE MIDDLE Ages the shrine of St Thomas Becket at Canterbury was the third most important shrine in Europe, after Rome and Santiago de Compostela. St Thomas's murder on the 29 December 1170 caused shock and outrage throughout England and beyond, but it also ushered in an extraordinary cult of devotion to the martyred archbishop who became a symbol of liberation against tyranny. Thanks to the extraordinary wealth of miracles worked through his intercession, he quickly became a refuge and advocate for the sick and afflicted. It is no exaggeration to say that Canterbury was a medieval Lourdes where instead of pilgrims immersing themselves in the waters of a spring, they made their way beneath the tomb of the martyr and prayed that grace would be poured down upon them.

St Thomas's inner life offered a powerful story. As his contemporaries were shocked at his death, some were not surprised—he had, after all, opposed the king; but God's response to his life, struggle and death shocked them even more. They were forced to ask themselves if they missed something. To them Thomas was ambitious, vain, materialistic, and rebellious; hardly the stuff of saints. Yet many of them did miss something: the process of conversion. One biographer notes that following Thomas's martyrdom one of his enemies, Richard de Lucy, was in conversation with one of the archbishop's former clerks, Henry of Houghton. Amazed at the devotion and tremendous cures that were won at Thomas's tomb, de Lucy wondered how it was all possible given Thomas's severe behaviour towards the Church as chancellor under Henry II. The clerk mused that Thomas had suffered almost seven years of exile, many injuries and then a cruel death; if St Peter and the Good Thief could obtain pardon for their sins, Thomas must surely have atoned for his lesser transgressions. Those years of hard exile and bitter suffering changed Thomas Becket.

The process of authentic conversion is rarely sudden, as it was with St Paul, it is usually more subtle and gradual. This was the case with Thomas. As he slowly woke to the way of true Christian discipleship, his experiences, his mistakes, his trials and sufferings, progressively turned him completely to Christ. The pilgrims who came to Canterbury were aware of this and as they asked his intercession they knew they were talking to a man who knew how hard life could be and how challenging the way of Christian discipleship can be.

Devotion to St Thomas Becket, or St Thomas of Canterbury as he is also known, cannot, in reality, be a sentimental affair; he was not a sentimental man, he was realist and even a combatant. Thomas cannot be dressed in sentimental piousness; rather he is a Saint (like all the Saints, truth be known) who deals with realities, difficulties and challenges, and this makes him a powerful intercessor. Thomas is a Saint for difficult times and afflicted people. He is a Saint for times when the Church is suffering and persecuted, when the powers and ideologies of the world seek to control her and the Gospel to their own advantage. Thomas is a Saint who, as he did in the moments before his martyrdom, stands to his full height and faces down the tyrant, the oppressors and the enemies of the Church; and he encourages his devotees to do the same. Henry VIII understood this all too clearly and was quick to destroy the shrine at Canterbury; but he could not destroy Thomas's legacy. We too, who now live in the greatest age of Christian martyrdom, who find the Church tossed about so violently on turbulent seas, perhaps even in danger of

Introduction xi

capsizing, should also understand this: St Thomas Becket is a Saint for our time and it is, perhaps, the time to renew our devotion to him.

This little book offers new devotions to St Thomas with the aim of encouraging Christians to rediscover this martyr's life and to count him among their companions on the pilgrim road we now walk. Among these devotions is a new novena for Christmas, beginning on Thomas's birthday and ending on his heavenly birthday—his *dies natalis*: the day of his martyrdom and feast day. There is also a programme for a pilgrimage to Canterbury based on the Catholic tradition of the Stations: this pilgrimage can be undertaken in the city itself, or spiritually at home or in one's local church. Other little prayers are offered for various needs: a new litany to the Saint, prayers for the sick, for the Church and for our priests.

When Thomas was invoked miracles were poured out upon the faithful, there is no reason to doubt that they can be again—physical miracles, yes, but perhaps also in this time, when the greatest afflictions are those of the mind, heart and soul, Thomas can be as effective in soothing the infirmities of modern men and women, many of whom suffer in silence and alienation: Thomas knows through his own experience of exile and isolation the sting and wounds of such suffering. He is a Saint for our times and for all times. May the Christian faithful find in him a good friend and advocate, and a wise teacher on our pilgrim path through this earthly city.

A Brief Life of St Thomas Becket

T Thomas Becket was born in Cheapside in London on the 21 December 1120, the son of Gilbert Becket and his wife Matilda. Of Norman ancestry, his father had been a textile merchant in Normandy, but had come to London to invest in property and the bulk of the family income came from rents. Thomas was one of four children born to the Beckets and the only son. His mother was his first teacher, teaching him to read and write while introducing him to basic arithmetic. A deeply pious woman, she also taught him the fundamentals of the Christian faith.

At the age of seven he was sent to the local parish school or "song school" where he improved upon his basic literacy skills. When he was ten his father enrolled him at the school at the Augustinian Merton Priory. There, Thomas had a classical education, learning Latin among other subjects. It was here that his singular talents were uncovered. Meanwhile, he was also engaging in middle-class pursuits mingling with his father's wealthy friends, being introduced to riding, hunting and hawking, games to which he would be devoted for most of his life.

When he was twenty he was sent to Paris to continue his education. For about two years the young scholar engaged in his studies and enjoyed the student life. However, when he was twenty-one, news that his mother had died reached him. Returning to London, Thomas bade farewell to his studies. Whether it was his intention to abandon his studies or not, his father's retirement and a series of misfortunes, including fires in a number of family properties, meant that the money was not there to send the young man back to Paris.

Thanks to his father's influence, after a year of lazing about, he found a position as a clerk in the business of a relative, Osbert Huitdeniers. In 1145, bored with his work, he was looking for a more interesting position. Setting his sights high, he gained a position in the employ of the Archbishop of Canterbury, Theobald of Bec. It was not long before the archbishop realized that he had a pearl in Thomas Becket and Theobald assigned him a tutor who instructed him in the knowledge he needed for work at an ecclesiastical court. With the young man's ability all too obvious, Theobald decided to send him to the continent to study canon law, enrolling him in the University of Bologna where Thomas spent a year, and then on to Auxerre to complete his studies.

When he returned to England he was entrusted with various missions for the archbishop and in each one he conducted himself admirably. Not long after this, the archbishop entrusted high office to his protégé: ordained deacon, he was appointed Archdeacon of Canterbury. He was now Theobald's right hand man, and apart from fulfilling various ecclesiastical duties, he was also at his archbishop's side during the negotiations to end the civil war, known as 'The Anarchy', which was devastating England. For his work in these talks Theobald dubbed Thomas "my first and only councillor". As Theobald led the negotiations to end the war between the Empress Matilda, daughter of the late King Henry I, and her cousin, King Stephen, for the English throne, Thomas's abilities and interventions not only helped reconciliation, but brought him to the attention of Matilda's son and the heir, Henry of Anjou. When Henry later succeeded as King Henry II in 1155, he asked Thomas to accept the office of

Royal Chancellor of England. The ambitious deacon agreed.

Now immersed in the affairs of state and living the life of a courtier, Thomas embraced the lifestyle his position brought. He wore fine clothing and ate well—he was known to be a lavish entertainer. He engaged in his favourite sports and he was by now accomplished in all of them. In his work he was as efficient and brilliant as before and the king benefited from his wise and capable service. A deep bond of friendship developed between Thomas and the king. While much has been made of a friendship between them it was never a relationship of equals: Thomas, in the king's eyes, was always a subject, albeit a close one. As the years passed, the character flaws of both men and their different view of things led to awkwardness and tensions.

For seven years Thomas served Henry as his royal minister. He managed the king's finances, raised taxes, carried out legal duties, served as power broker, peacemaker, negotiator and pacifier of Henry's wrath. He also served the king and his family on a personal basis, welcoming the king's son Henry into his household as a foster son according to the medieval custom of tutorship. Sent on diplomatic missions, he astounded people with his entourage and grand table, so much so many wondered how great his king must be if the chancellor could travel with such grandeur. He was even involved in Henry's military exploits, leading his own knights in various battles in France. It was during one of these, at a council of war during the siege of Toulouse, that Thomas and Henry had their first bitter quarrel. This quarrel would be the first of many, and Henry wisely noted that his chancellor did not back down from an argument easily.

While Thomas's personal life at this time was not exactly exemplary—he had done wrong for the sake of his king, as some of his contemporaries noted, he maintained the piety his mother had taught him. He prayed regularly and took the discipline now and again. He was devout, and, most importantly of all, he was chaste. Though Henry had, at times, tried to trap his chancellor into sexual sin with some of the women that frequented the court, Thomas always resisted and often fled the scene.

In 1160 Theobald of Bec fell ill, dying on the 18 April 1161. His relationship with Thomas had soured in the last years of his life due to some of Thomas's fiscal decisions which had imposed taxes on the Church and limited some of the Church's rights and freedoms. For a year Henry did not permit a successor to Theobald to be elected, he wanted to benefit from the income of Canterbury while the See was vacant. But the king knew who he wanted to succeed the feisty archbishop. Henry had designs on the Church and meant to have his way; he needed a loyal subject in the office: that minion was to be Thomas.

Henry thought he had put Thomas in his place after their quarrel at the council of war; this gave him the confidence to suggest to his chancellor that he should succeed Theobald. Thomas was horrified: he realized that the office of the primate deserved a more religious and saintly man and he was not suited. As Henry continued to make advances, Thomas was broken down. With the "assistance" of the king's barons, the monastic chapter elected Thomas archbishop and the decision was ratified at a council of clergy and noblemen at Westminster Abbey on the 23 May 1162. On the 2 June he was ordained a priest at Canterbury Cathedral, and the following day he was consecrated archbishop.

A Brief Life of St Thomas Becket

St Thomas is enthroned as Archbishop of Canterbury

Now Primate of England and chief shepherd of the kingdom's Christians, something happened to Thomas Becket at this time; it has been called his conversion. At his ordination he recognised that as a priest and bishop, the shepherd of the flock, he could no longer conspire with his king to hand the rights, freedoms and treasures of the Church to the state. He was no longer content to comply with the king's demands or compromise his integrity and faith. Having waited for four months after his consecration, in the autumn of 1162 he resigned as chancellor. He did not consult the king nor ask his permission and this was a shock to Henry. When the letter of resignation arrived the king was furious and launched into an attack on the new archbishop: in Henry's eyes Becket had betrayed him.

The new archbishop had begun as he meant to go on. As Henry seethed over the resignation, Thomas was working out how he was going to recover the property and castles the barons, with Henry's blessing, had, in his view, stolen from the Church. The stage was set for another civil war in England, this time between Church and state.

Thomas's personal life gradually changed in the first years of his administration. His life of simple piety yielded to a more intense living of the Gospel. While he had prayed before, now he gave more time to meditation and conversation with God. He offered night vigils, seeking guidance and help from the Lord as he engaged in the controversies that accompanied his defence of the Church and her rights. He continued to take the discipline, but now he also adopted the practice of wearing a hairshirt beneath his clothes. Externally, he still wore fine clothes, and though they were the vesture of his office, they were made of silk and other fine materials; he would gradually dispense with the finery and wear simple, dark clothes. He continued to entertain well: he understood that as archbishop and primate it was expected that he should do so, but office apart, he still liked his finery at table.

As archbishop he realized he needed a better grasp of theology and engaged a tutor to teach him. He discovered a great interest in Scripture, and devoted a lot of time to studying it, together with works of theology, philosophy, canon and civil law, and devotional works. Though more devout, Thomas was still the skilled politician, very much aware that a serious war lay ahead and he was determined to win whatever battles he had to fight with Henry.

He got to work immediately and before long, archbishop and king clashed. First of all Thomas wanted an end to the practice whereby the king benefited from the income from vacant Sees. Kings had delayed appointing bishops, leaving the faithful without a shepherd while the state took the income; this had to come to an end. Secondly, Thomas refused to allow clerics be tried in secular courts but rather face any charge made against them in ecclesiastical courts according to canon law. The issue of a tax called "sheriffs' aid" also occupied him: he repudiated the mandatory nature of this payment and suggested that the Church make a voluntary offering instead. Coupled with his campaign on these issues, he was also quite successful in recovering Church property and insisting upon Church rights and freedoms.

Henry was growing impatient and he realized that his new archbishop had to be dealt with, complaining to whoever would listen that Thomas was undermining his authority and rights as sovereign. At a meeting at the king's palace at Woodstock in July 1163 many of these issues were raised, in particular the "sheriffs' aid", and led to a heated argument which Thomas won. Not content to let the archbishop triumph over him, in October of that year, Henry summoned the bishops to Westminster to hear his complaints about the Church's refusal to accept what he called the ancestral customs, practices that undermined the Church's liberty and gave the king governing power over ecclesiastical affairs. The bishops stood behind Thomas and refused to agree to any custom that conflicted with canon law.

Henry realized he had to use other means to bring his difficult archbishop into line. He withdrew his son Henry from Thomas's household, a sign that he had lost the royal favour. The king also began to foster alliances among some of the bishops who found Thomas a little too highhanded for their liking. Both Thomas and Henry petitioned the pope for support, but Pope Alexander III decided to occupy the middle ground and urged compromise: he had political problems of his own as he tried to oust an anti-pope and battle the Holy Roman Emperor, Frederick Barbarossa. Sensing he might need a safe haven, Thomas began to make contacts in Europe to secure refuge should he be forced into exile.

In January 1164 Henry summoned the bishops to Clarendon Palace in Wiltshire. There he pressed upon them an undertaking that the bishops would uphold his rights and swear to adhere to the ancestral customs that had been established with regard to monarch's relationship with the Church. While Thomas initially refused to consent, after much debate and threats, he relented and a charter of these customs, the Constitutions of Clarendon, was formulated. Tricked into accepting them, Thomas fell into spiritual darkness and adopted an extreme penitential regime in atonement for his failures. He soon fell afoul of the agreement when, in August of that year, he tried to travel to France without the king's permission. Arrested, he was put on trial for other charges and found guilty. The king added insult to injury as he laid more charges against the archbishop, these concerned his spending as chancellor and his refusal to fulfil his oath as required by the Constitutions of Clarendon. Thomas refused to engage with the charges and was found guilty. He realised the time had come for him to go into exile. In November 1164 he fled to France.

For the next six years Thomas lived in France, engaging with Henry from a distance in the war for the Church's rights and freedom. His property and benefices were confiscated, as were those of the clerks who had accompanied him into exile; members of Thomas's family and those of his clerks were also exiled. While Henry sought to punish the English members of the religious orders that gave Thomas shelter, he could not touch the archbishop as King Louis VII of France had taken him under his protection. In those years Thomas wrote numerous letters to bishops, noblemen and the pope to seek their support and resolve the dispute. The pope continued to counsel the archbishop not to provoke Henry. Thomas had only one weapon left in his arsenal: censure. In the spring of 1165 he warned Henry that if he did not settle with him, censures would be imposed. Henry ignored him. When the pope conferred on Thomas the status of papal legate, he knew he had what he needed. At Pentecost 1166 while on pilgrimage to the Abbey of Vézelay, the shrine of St Mary Magdalen, Thomas excommunicated a number of Henry's advisors and supporters, including a bishop: Jocelin de Bohon, the Bishop of Salisbury, one of Henry's ardent clerical advisors.

St Thomas confronts King Henry II

The excommunications brought matters to a head, and Pope Alexander was forced to get involved. Papal representatives went back and forward trying to find solutions, but as the dispute raged on, and one intrigue led to another, both Henry and Thomas hardened in their positions. This put the pope in a difficult position; while he understood Thomas's position and supported it privately, he needed the English king's backing in his own dispute with the German emperor. However by 1170 the pope managed to eke out a compromise with Henry, facilitating Thomas's return to England in November of that year.

However, another issue emerged: that of the coronation of young Prince Henry as junior king; as Archbishop of Canterbury, Thomas had the right to crown kings. In June 1170 King Henry had the Archbishop of York crown his son, thus infringing Thomas's rights. In response, with the permission of the pope, Thomas laid an interdict on England and excommunicated the bishops involved in the ceremony: Roger, Archbishop of York, and two assisting bishops, Bishop Gilbert Foliot of London and Bishop Jocelin of Salisbury. More negotiations followed, led by the pope and they reached a resolution. The interdict was lifted and Henry agreed to compromise. However, while Thomas agreed to absolve the two assisting bishops, he refused to lift the excommunication of the Archbishop of York saying that only the pope could do so.

In the meantime he returned to Canterbury at the end of November 1170. As he travelled the roads to Canterbury, crowds of the faithful came out to see him and hail him as a victor. They may have been indifferent to his election, but his heroism in fighting Henry, whom most now saw as a tyrant, endeared him to the people. Back in Canterbury, Thomas settled down to celebrate Christmas with his monks. He preached at the Christmas Day Mass in the cathedral, telling the faithful that his time with them would be short—the time of his death was near: Canterbury would soon have a new martyr, he told them. The people were stunned and many of them left the Mass in tears. Meanwhile the Archbishop of York sent delegates to Normandy to plead his case with Henry. The king was furious with what he perceived was Thomas's obstinacy in refusing to lift the excommunication, and in full court he denounced Thomas as ungrateful. Four of his knights, Reginald fitzUrse, Hugh de Moville, William de Tracy and Richard le Breton, took note. Leaving the court, they made for a ship to take them to England to relieve their sovereign of his disloyal subject.

The knights arrived at Canterbury in the afternoon of the 29 December 1170. Thomas granted them a meeting at which he was accused by the knights of disloyalty to the king. He once again explained why he could not lift the excommunication; the matter was in the pope's hands. Threatening him with death, the knights accused him of treason before leaving the meeting, not to return to the king but to fetch their weapons which they had left outside.

Thomas made his way to the cathedral for Vespers. When some monks suggested barricading the door for fear of the knights' return, Thomas told them to leave it open—the church was not to be made a citadel. The knights returned, brandishing their swords, calling for the archbishop. As monks and clerics fled to safety, Thomas came forward to confront them, forbidding the knights from harming the clergy and people. The four attacked him with their swords. When he had fallen to the floor, one of the knights struck his head, slicing off the crown of his skull. A fifth attacker scattered the archbishop's brains across the paving with this swords. The knights then fled.

The canons and monks, in a state of confusion and horror, closed the cathedral, and then spent the night in vigil before Thomas's body. It was decided to bury him quickly. The unwashed body was undressed, revealing his hairshirt and the marks of his penances, and then vested in episcopal vestments and interred. There was no Requiem Mass because the cathedral was in a state of desecration.

News of the killing quickly spread from Canterbury to all of England and beyond; all Europe was shocked. Many spoke of his death as martyrdom and miracles began to occur when he was invoked. A little more than two years after his death Thomas was canonized a Saint on the 21 February 1173 by Pope Alexander. Henry was formally chastised and the knights excommunicated. On the 12 July 1173 the king came on a penitential pilgrimage to the tomb of the archbishop and there did public penance for his part in the assassination. On the 7 July 1220 the saint's body was translated to a new, more splendid tomb and this became the focus of pilgrimage for the next three hundred years as miracles continued to occur. Canterbury became one of the most important pilgrimage sites in Europe, and Thomas became a potent symbol for the Church in her struggle with the secular powers for her rights and freedom.

Christmas Novena to St Thomas Becket

Day 1: 21 December

On this day St Thomas was born in London, 1120.

'Blessed is she who believed that the promise made her by the Lord would be fulfilled' (Lk 1:45)

Reflection

ND SO St Thomas returned to Canterbury after six years of exile. An uneasy reconciliation now existed between him and the king. But Thomas knew it would not last. In his heart he understood his fight for the Church's rights and freedom might only be resolved in the shedding of blood: his blood. Yet he returned to his flock and to his cathedral, ready to embrace whatever sacrifice was required. In faith, he put his life into the hands of Christ his Saviour. He knew he would not be confounded, for Christ was all in all.

Novena Prayers

Blessed Thomas, in your kindness, intercede with the Lord, that he may grant me a deeper faith and a greater trust in him. So rooted in Christ, may I believe that the promises he made to us will be fulfilled. May his coming at Christmas banish my fears and anxieties, immerse me in the light of his holy Incarnation and make me a true witness to the Gospel.

Pray, St Thomas, for these intentions which I now lay before you …

Rejoice, O holy Archbishop, rejoice; for after the visitation of the Divine Child, you shall be born in Him, an infant in the Kingdom of Heaven.

And blessed are those who believe, for they shall shine like bright stars in the midst of winter, bringing warmth and light. O light in the midst of darkness, St Thomas, lead us to the eternal light of Christ our Lord.

Rejoice, O holy Archbishop, rejoice; for after the visitation of the Divine Child, you shall be born in Him, an infant in the Kingdom of Heaven.

Almighty and eternal God, your martyr, St Thomas Becket, confirmed the depths of his faith through the shedding of his blood. Through his intercession, grant your people a renewal in this virtue, that they may reveal your loving kindness through their fidelity.
We ask this through Christ our Lord. Amen.

DAY 2: 22 DECEMBER

'My soul proclaims the greatness of the Lord' (Lk 1:46)

Reflection

Though lured by the attractions of the world and stately power, St Thomas did not completely abandon the simple piety of his youth. His mother, Matilda, was his first teacher in prayer, and each day he faithfully offered praise to the Lord. Following his conversion he spent hours in prayer, offering vigils at night in praise of God. In the midst of his trials he found great consolation in proclaiming the greatness of God. It was as he was making his way to Vespers that he was struck down by his enemies, but he made of his death an act of praise to God. Since then, his blood, rather than crying out for vengeance, has sought to urge all Christ's people to fervent devotion.

Novena Prayers

St Thomas, fervent servant of the Lord, teach me the way of prayer that I may offer to the Lord a true sacrifice of praise, in thanksgiving for his wonders in my life, and in testament to the love which unites us to him. May his coming at Christmas inspire me to devote my life to the praise of his glory. May I proclaim his greatness among the peoples.

Pray, St Thomas, for these intentions which I now lay before you …

Rejoice, O holy Archbishop, rejoice; for after the visitation of the Divine Child, you shall be born in Him, an infant in the Kingdom of Heaven.

And blessed are those who praise the Lord, for like a great trees, they will bear fruit in abundance. O living Psalm of Christ, St Thomas, lead us in that great canticle of praise, the holy work of God, which fills all heaven with the praise of the Most High.

Rejoice, O holy Archbishop, rejoice; for after the visitation of the Divine Child, you shall be born in Him, an infant in the Kingdom of Heaven.

Lord Jesus Christ, who when on earth spent long nights in prayer to your Eternal Father; through the intercession of your martyr, St Thomas Becket, grant us the gift of a sincere and fulsome prayer, that we your disciples may, through constant praise, transform this earth into a cenacle of true devotion. Who lives and reigns with God the Father in the unity of the Holy Spirit, one God, for ever and ever. Amen.

DAY 3: 23 DECEMBER

'"What will this child turn out to be?" they wondered. And indeed the hand of the Lord was with him.' (Lk 1:66)

Reflection

An ambitious young man, St Thomas sought worldly preferment, and this ambition was satisfied as he rose through the ranks to become Royal Chancellor of England. His election as Archbishop shocked him. He did not see himself as religious or saintly enough for such an office. However, it seemed to open a new reality for him—the providence of God. It not was king or benefactors which brought him to this office, but, in a mysterious way, God himself. St Thomas's conversion seems to have been effected by the realization that the hand of God was upon him and that now he must forget self and become the Lord's servant for the good of the Church.

Novena Prayers

St Thomas, you abandoned your worldly ambitions when the Lord raised you to be the Primate of the English, entrusting the souls of his people to your care. As shepherd, you offered yourself to protect them and the Church, even to the shedding of your blood. May Christ's coming at Christmas in obedience to the Father, lead me to abandon myself to the will of God that his providence may guide my life and make of me a sacrifice acceptable to him.

Intercede, dear St Thomas, for these intentions which I now entrust to you ...

Rejoice, O holy Archbishop, rejoice; for after the visitation of the Divine Child, you shall be born in Him, an infant in the Kingdom of Heaven.

And blessed are those who abandon themselves in to the hands of the Eternal Father, for totally his, they shall work wonders in the sight of all peoples. O true servant of the Lamb, St Thomas, lead us to offer ourselves as an oblation to the Lord.

Rejoice, O holy Archbishop, rejoice; for after the visitation of the Divine Child, you shall be born in Him, an infant in the Kingdom of Heaven.

Almighty and eternal God, whose martyr, St Thomas Becket, renounced his desires and worldly ambitions to place his entire life at your service for love of you and for the salvation of souls; through his intercession, grant that we, your children, may with confidence abandon yourselves to your holy will. We ask this through Christ our Lord. Amen.

DAY 4: 24 DECEMBER

'And you, little child, you shall be called Prophet of the Most High.' (Lk 1:76)

Reflection

It was the will of God that St Thomas should be a prophet. He was by no means perfect, indeed in many of his actions, even as Archbishop, he compromised his prophetic call. He was often angry and impulsive. His battles with King Henry brought out the worst in him. Yet, overall, and in the end, he was a noble prophet who challenged the world by reiterating the primacy of God's law. His heroic death was that of a prophet, of one who was willing to lay down his life for the truth he preached. St Thomas was, in his day, another John the Baptist. Every age needs such figures, including our own.

Novena Prayers

St Thomas, devoted prophet of the Lord, you embraced the truth of the Gospel and the primacy of Christ's kingdom even in this world, shedding your blood, like St John the Baptist, as a wonderful testimony. May the Lord's coming at Christmas fill me with a similar heroism, that rejoicing at singular mystery of his Incarnation, I may speak with a prophetic voice the truths he has taught us.

Intercede, dear St Thomas, for these intentions which I now entrust to you …

Rejoice, O holy Archbishop, rejoice; for after the visitation of the Divine Child, you shall be born in Him, an infant in the Kingdom of Heaven.

And blessed are those who, with heroic hearts, fearlessly proclaim the Gospel of the Lord even to the shedding of their blood, for God himself will be their inheritance. O fearless Voice crying throughout our land, beloved St Thomas, lead us to embrace our baptismal call to be prophets of God the Most High.

Rejoice, O holy Archbishop, rejoice; for after the visitation of the Divine Child, you shall be born in Him, an infant in the Kingdom of Heaven.

Eternal Father, who raised your martyr, St Thomas Becket, from a life of worldly comforts to stand among the prophets of your Church and proclaim your truth in the midst of the world, strengthening him in the face of oppression and suffering; through his intercession grant your children every grace that they too may fearlessly live and proclaim your Gospel even in the midst of great trial. We ask this through Christ our Lord. Amen.

DAY 5: 25 DECEMBER

On this day God-made-man, the Saviour of the world, was born in Bethlehem.

'The Word was made flesh, he lived among us' (Jn 1:14)

Reflection

That last Christmas, celebrated in the cathedral not long after he returned from exile, St Thomas preached to his people. The shepherd had been restored to proclaim the sacred mysteries to the flock entrusted to his care. As they listened to him, as they looked at him, his people rejoiced in his presence and thanked God for his being given back to them. They may have been indifferent at his appointment, but his heroic defence of their Church and his growth in holiness had endeared him to their hearts. They had lined the streets to welcome him back. Now their joy reached fulfilment as they shared the Holy Eucharist with him. In his person, they see one like Christ. On that Christmas, as they contemplate with him the mystery of the Incarnation, they see in their holy Archbishop, Christ dwelling among them.

Novena Prayers

Blessed Thomas, in you we see Christ. In you we see the one who comes into our midst to proclaim liberation to captives and joy to the downtrodden. In you *in persona Christi capitis* as priest and bishop, Christ is present among us to console us. At his coming on this Christmas day, intercede that I may rejoice in his presence, and as a member of his Body the Church, seek to make him present to the men and women of our time.

Pray, St Thomas, for these intentions which I now lay before you ...

Rejoice, O holy Archbishop, rejoice; for after the visitation of the Divine Child, you shall be born in Him, an infant in the Kingdom of Heaven.

And blessed are those who, through holy lives, make present in their flesh our beloved Lord and Saviour Jesus Christ, for the vision of God shines through them. O holy priest of Christ, St Thomas, lead us to the Word made flesh that he may transform us with his heavenly grace.

Rejoice, O holy Archbishop, rejoice; for after the visitation of the Divine Child, you shall be born in Him, an infant in the Kingdom of Heaven.

Wondrous Child, Lord Jesus, in your birth you bring life; to winter, spring; to snow, thaw; to darkness, light; to a people starved for redemption, the bread of salvation. Through the intercession of your martyr, St Thomas, transform your people in the mystery of the Incarnation, that through holy lives, they may, in their flesh, make you present to the men and women of our time. Amen.

DAY 6: 26 DECEMBER

On this day the blessed Stephen was the first to lay down his life for Christ.

'Do not worry about how to speak or what to say; what you are to say will be given to you when the time comes.'
(Mt 10:19)

Reflection

A time came for St Thomas when he realized that neither exile nor law, be it the law of the Church or the law of the land, could save him. Now the time had come to trust in the Lord. What he was to do next, what he was to say, it was not up to him to decide. Rather, like an empty vessel, he had to place himself before the Fountain of grace and receive what the Lord had for him. His ascetic life led him to this insight. His love of God strengthened him, his prayer and long night vigils opened his heart. Like St Stephen he was ready to endure what he had to endure to fulfil the will of God. Like Stephen, he committed himself into the hands of Christ.

Novena Prayers

St Thomas, you cast aside fear to embrace that heroism which is found in complete trust in God. With an open heart you awaited the promptings of grace. Through Christ's coming at Christmas, pray dear Saint, that I too will place my trust in him, for he who was made flesh for our sake is with us.

Pray, St Thomas, for these intentions which I now lay before you …

Rejoice, O holy Archbishop, rejoice; for after the visitation of the Divine Child, you shall be born in Him, an infant in the Kingdom of Heaven.

And blessed are those who trust in the Lord and take refuge in him, for like living streams they water the earth with peace. O holy Ark, St Thomas, refuge for those who invoke you, lead us to the merciful Heart of Jesus—to our Shelter, to our Refuge, to our eternal joy.

Rejoice, O holy Archbishop, rejoice; for after the visitation of the Divine Child, you shall be born in Him, an infant in the Kingdom of Heaven.

Eternal Wisdom, Son of the Father, Son of Man, Lord Jesus, you consoled your servant, St Thomas Becket with your grace, leading him to entrust himself to your mercy; through his intercession grant us the grace to overcome all anxiety, and with patience and confidence, entrust ourselves wholeheartedly to you. Who lives and reigns for ever and ever. Amen

DAY 7: 27 DECEMBER

On this day Holy John the Apostle gazed once again on the Face of his Beloved.

'That life was made visible: we saw it and we are giving our testimony' (1 Jn 1:2)

Reflection

Following his election as Archbishop, St Thomas's ordination as priest affected him deeply. It may well have been the moment of his conversion. Having served as a deacon up to this point, his worldly ways seemed unaffected by the call to diaconal service. But sharing in the ministerial priesthood, in the priesthood of Christ, opened a new horizon to him. Now he must be true to his ordination. Now he must offer his life in testimony to the Word of God made Man and to his sacrifice, celebrated each day in the Mass. The life of Christ was now so real it was part of him as a priest. If he stayed silent, the very stones would be urged to cry out! But there was no need; the stones could be at peace. Thomas would now speak.

Novena Prayers

Blessed priest of the Lord, St Thomas, at your ordination the grace of the sacrament opened your eyes to the reality of your calling. Like St John the Beloved Disciple, you saw and you believed, and you gave testimony. In your struggle with King Henry, you had a deep concern for his soul and sought to lead him to Christ. Through the Lord's coming at Christmas, pray that I may not remain silent, but true to my baptismal calling proclaim the Gospel in my life and do what I can to lead souls to Christ.

Intercede, dear St Thomas, for these intentions which I now entrust to you ...

Rejoice, O holy Archbishop, rejoice; for after the visitation of the Divine Child, you shall be born in Him, an infant in the Kingdom of Heaven.

And blessed are those who proclaim the word of the Lord from the housetops, for they like the blowing of the wind, shall cover the earth, refreshing the hearts of all peoples. O living Testimony of truth, St Thomas, lead us to the wisdom of God.

Rejoice, O holy Archbishop, rejoice; for after the visitation of the Divine Child, you shall be born in Him, an infant in the Kingdom of Heaven.

Heavenly Father, from whom comes all truth and all that is good, through the intercession of your martyr, St Thomas Becket, who made of his priestly life a living testimony to your Gospel, confirm us in the truth and inspire us to proclaim that same Gospel with courage and fervour. We ask this through Christ our Lord. Amen.

DAY 8: 28 DECEMBER

On this day the Holy Innocents of Bethlehem fell beneath the sword of Herod but were raised with Christ.

'God is light; there is no darkness in him at all.' (1 Jn 1:5)

Reflection

St Thomas faced many demons. His ordinary temptations gave way to the greater ones that plague the faithful ministers of the Lord. Finally, he was assailed by those that urged him to renounce his office and also by those that counselled him to stand firm but with pride. He was tempted to be distracted by the working of evil around him, unchristian conspiracy, disloyalty, faithlessness, fear and weakness. He had one refuge: Christ, and he humbly took shelter in him. When the time came, not even the fear of death could shake him. The power of the evil one had been dispelled by the light of Christ.

Novena Prayers

St Thomas, for centuries you have been renowned as one who protects the weak and poor, who brings consolation and healing to the sick, who counsels those in need of God's wisdom. Hear my prayers, blessed martyr, that at the coming of my Saviour at Christmas, I may rejoice in the protection he brings, dispelling the darkness and saving me from the power of the evil one. Be my protector, St Thomas, that I may rejoice in the salvation Christ has won for me.

Intercede, dear St Thomas, for these intentions which I now entrust to you ...

Rejoice, O holy Archbishop, rejoice; for after the visitation of the Divine Child, you shall be born in Him, an infant in the Kingdom of Heaven.

And blessed are those who share in Christ's victory over sin and death, for even the demons shall flee from their holy presence. O Knight of the living God, St Thomas, our protector, lead us through the darkness of this world with the light of Christ aflame in our hearts.

Rejoice, O holy Archbishop, rejoice; for after the visitation of the Divine Child, you shall be born in Him, an infant in the Kingdom of Heaven.

All powerful and ever living God, in your gracious mercy you raise your people from the darkness of sin and death, dispelling the power of the evil one. Through the intercession of your martyr, St Thomas Becket who, by your grace, triumphed through the shedding of his blood, assist your children in their daily struggles with evil and temptation. We ask this through Christ our Lord. Amen.

DAY 9: 29 DECEMBER

On this day the blessed Thomas was born into eternal life, 1170.

'You are the men who have stood by me faithfully in my trials; and now I confer a kingdom on you.' (Lk 22:28-29)

Reflection

After an altercation with Henry's knights, as they departed, St Thomas made his way to the cathedral for Vespers. In prayer he would find consolation and strength. But they were waiting for him, and in his own cathedral, not far from the altar, they struck him down and his blood poured out on to the flagstones. As the knights fled, the monks, in horror, ran to assist their Archbishop, but the Lord had taken him. It was Thomas who would now assist them and all who would come to his tomb. What Thomas had renounced in spirit, he renounced in the flesh; what he had lost, he now regained with much interest. He lost his life for Christ, and now Christ crowns him with eternal life and confers a kingdom on him. The man dies; the martyr-saint and advocate for the faithful is born.

Novena Prayers

Glorious St Thomas, faithful martyr, prince of Christ's kingdom, I greet you and bless you on this holy day, for the Lord has done great and mighty things for you. For the shedding of your blood, he has made you an advocate and intercessor for all his people, and so I turn to you and ask your kind intercession. Through Christ's coming at Christmas, pray that like you, I too may renounce myself, take up my cross and follow him. May I stand faithfully by him, not for any reward he has promised, but for the sake of love. Pray, O Blessed Thomas, that I may love him with all my heart.

And pray, dear St Thomas, for these intentions which I now entrust to you …

Rejoice, O holy Archbishop, rejoice; for after the visitation of the Divine Child, you shall be born in Him, an infant in the Kingdom of Heaven.

And blessed are those who have given up their lives for the sake of Christ, for now they reign with him in his eternal kingdom. O Blessed Martyr of God, St Thomas, lead us on the way of renunciation so we may one day delight in the eternal Vision of his Face.

Rejoice, O holy Archbishop, rejoice; for after the visitation of the Divine Child, you shall be born in Him, an infant in the Kingdom of Heaven.

Almighty and Eternal God, you gave your blessed martyr St Thomas Becket, the grace to renounce earthly fear so to be faithful unto death. Grant us, we pray, through his intercession, that we your people may eschew all worldly honour, and embracing what is right and true, bear witness to your eternal kingdom. One day, may we come to share with him in the life you have prepared for your faithful. We ask this through Christ our Lord. Amen.

Festal Invocations in Honour of St Thomas Becket

WE PRAISE YOU, O God,
for in your mercy, you raise up your faithful servant, Thomas;
St Thomas, son of the Church, *pray for us.*

We praise you, O God,
for you touched the heart of your disciple Thomas and converted him;
St Thomas, pastor of Canterbury, *pray for us.*

We praise you, O God,
for you drew him into the furnace of your charity;
St Thomas, made poor among poor, *pray for us.*

We praise you, O God,
for you opened his eyes to your Holy Gospel and immersed him in your Word;
St Thomas, Beatitude in the flesh, *pray for us.*

We praise you, O God,
for you granted him the courage to defy the tyrant;
St Thomas, humble in fortitude, *pray for us.*

We praise you, O God,
for you led him to triumph over his weakness and sinfulness;
St Thomas, penitent and meek, *pray for us.*

We praise you, O God,
for in exile you moulded him into a citizen of your kingdom;
St Thomas, child reigning in the heavens, *pray for us.*

We praise you, O God,
For you made him the defender of the poor and the oppressed;
St Thomas, protector of the rights of the downtrodden, *pray for us*

We praise you, O God,
for you crowned him with faith and hope in the midst of his trials;
St Thomas, rooted in the virtues of Christ, *pray for us.*

We praise you, O God,
for you gave him the grace to triumph over suffering and death;
St Thomas, obedient to the will of the Father, *pray for us.*

We praise you, O God,
for you crowned your servant, Thomas, with the grace of holy martyrdom;
St Thomas, united in victory with the death of Christ, *pray for us.*

We praise you, O God,
For through the intercession of your blessed servant you pour out miracles;
St Thomas, advocate for all people, *pray for us.*

V. Pray for us, O Blessed Thomas, faithful martyr of the Lord;
R. That we may be made worthy of the promises of Christ.

Let us pray:

We praise you, O God,
for in your servant, St Thomas Becket,
you give your people a powerful advocate in their needs
and a companion on the pilgrimage of life.
Hear his prayers on our behalf,
and through his example and intercession,
strengthen us in our daily living of the Gospel
so we too may attain the blessings
he has won for his fidelity to Christ.
We ask this through the same Christ our Lord.
Amen.

St Thomas and Pope Alexander bid farewell

Various Prayers to St Thomas

PILGRIM PRAYER TO ST THOMAS BECKET

V. To you, glorious St Thomas, I offer my prayer;
R. May the Lord hear your prayers for those who invoke you.
V. O blessed Primate, whose blood was poured out for Christ,
R. May the Lord hear your prayers for those who invoke you.

O holy St Thomas, faithful bishop of the Lord, you learned humility and virtue from the graces God conferred on you, leading you to defend the Church and her people in the face of tyranny. You bowed your head to receive the blow and crown of martyrdom, offering your life and death for Christ's Church and the cause of peace and reconciliation. Hear my prayers, and help me embrace the Gospel in my daily life, seeking holiness and joyfully carrying the cross God in his wisdom has permitted for me. Obtain for me the virtue of fortitude so as a true disciple I may be a faithful witness to Christ in the world and my life may be pleasing to him. Be my companion on my pilgrim path and guide me with your wisdom so I may better understand the way the Lord has laid out for me. Pray, that one day I shall stand with you in the eternal kingdom in company with the Virgin Mary and with all the Saints in the presence of our loving God. Amen.

V. Pray for us, O blessed Thomas, martyr of the Church:
R. That we may be made worthy of the promises of Christ.

Let us pray:

Almighty Father, strengthened by your grace your martyr, St Thomas Becket, laid down his life with courage and faith in defence of the Church, trusting in your promise that all who lose their lives for Christ's sake will find life. Through his intercession help us to deny ourselves for Christ's sake in this life to find that place he has prepared for us in your eternal kingdom. Through Christ our Lord. Amen.

MEMORARE TO ST THOMAS BECKET

Remember, O most blessed martyr, Thomas,
that as you endured exile and suffering
in defence of holy Mother Church,
you appealed to the Lord in your distress
and he did not abandon you
but sustained you in your needs.
So hear me now, O sweet Servant of God,
intercede with Christ for me
that he may sustain me in my trials
and pour out his manifold graces upon me.
O Fountain of Miracles, O Almoner of Graces,
do not refuse to listen to my prayers
but in your kindness hearken to my pleas.
Amen.

Novena for the Grace of Conversion

Through the Intercession of St Thomas Becket

O Jesus, you have urged us: "Unless you become like little children, you shall not enter the kingdom of heaven". Lord, help me die to myself and embrace the way of spiritual childhood so your grace may triumph in me, and my heart turn to your ways. This I ask through the intercession of your martyr St Thomas, who through suffering and exile found the way of humility.
Say the Our Father, one Hail Mary and the Glory be.
St Thomas Becket, pray for us.

O Jesus, you have told us: "If you wish to be a disciple of mine, you must renounce yourself, take up your cross and follow me". Lord, help me to be forgetful of myself and with true humility embrace the way of cross so you may teach me true discipleship and I may grow in charity. This I ask through the intercession of St Thomas, who through trials and humiliation learned the way of sacrifice.
Say the Our Father, one Hail Mary and the Glory be.
St Thomas Becket, pray for us.

O Jesus, you have commanded us: "Love one another as I have loved you". Lord, help me to turn away from my love of self to embrace the way of selfless love so you may transform me into an oblation to be offered in your service and the service of my brothers and sisters. This I ask through the intercession of St Thomas, who through his sacrifice to death was made an offering for peace and reconciliation.

Say the Our Father, one Hail Mary and the Glory be.
St Thomas Becket, pray for us.

O Lord Jesus Christ who by your grace and mercy transform souls and make them holy, hear my prayers and turn my heart to you so I may be wholly converted to the will of the Eternal Father and the way of Christian discipleship. Form me according to your Sacred Heart and make your designs and desires my own. May my life be immersed in yours so I may truly say, "I live, now, not I, but Christ lives in me". Grant this through the prayers of your Immaculate Mother Mary and your faithful martyr, Thomas. Amen.

Hail, holy Queen, Mother of mercy,
hail, our life, our sweetness, and our hope.
To you we cry, the children of Eve;
to you we send up our sighs,
mourning and weeping in this land of exile.
Turn, then, most gracious advocate,
your eyes of mercy toward us;
lead us home at last
and show us the blessed fruit of your womb, Jesus:
O clement, O loving, O sweet Virgin Mary.

St Thomas Becket, pray for us.

Prayer of the Sick to St Thomas Becket

O great Saint of Miracles, dear St Thomas,
I place myself under your fatherly care
and beg that you may obtain for me
the miracles of healing so many received
when they had recourse to you.
Ask our Blessed Saviour to pour out upon me,
from the sacred wounds of his passion,
his soothing grace to ease my suffering
and if it be his will, to grant me a cure.
But if I must carry this cross,
then, sweet Thomas, help me embrace it
and to rejoice in uniting it with Christ's,
and with all he bore for the salvation of souls.
O blessed Thomas, let me now take shelter
beneath the Ark of your intercession,
there may I find peace and strength,
and the joy of knowing the power of Christ's love.
Amen.

St Thomas falls ill after his penances

Litany for the Sick

Through the Intercession of St Thomas of Canterbury

Lord Jesus, the ones whom you love are sick:
grant them your peace and your healing.
Through the prayers of your holy martyr Thomas:
grant them your peace and your healing.
Through the merits of his conversion to grace:
grant them your peace and your healing.
Through the merits of his dying to self:
grant them your peace and your healing.
Through the merits of his faithful service as Shepherd:
grant them your peace and your healing.
Through the merits of his love for the Holy Eucharist:
grant them your peace and your healing.
Through the merits of his defence of the Church:
grant them your peace and your healing.
Through the merits of his courage:
grant them your peace and your healing.
Through the merits of his suffering:
grant them your peace and your healing.
Through the merits of the exile he endured for your Church:
grant them your peace and your healing.
Through the merits of his penance and self-denial:
grant them your peace and your healing.
Through the merits of his ardent prayer:
grant them your peace and your healing.
Through the merits of his love for his brethren:
grant them your peace and your healing.
Through the merits of his charity to the poor:

grant them your peace and your healing.
Through the merits of his fearless preaching:
grant them your peace and your healing.
Through the merits of his obedience to holy Mother Church:
grant them your peace and your healing.
Through the merits of his trust in you:
grant them your peace and your healing.
Through the merits of his long night vigils:
grant them your peace and your healing.
Through the merits of his patience and longsuffering:
grant them your peace and your healing.
Through the merits of his total offering of self:
grant them your peace and your healing.
Through the merits of his martyr's death:
grant them your peace and your healing.
Through the merits of his faithful love:
grant them your peace and your healing.
Lord Jesus, the ones whom you love are sick;
through the intercession of your faithful martyr Thomas:
grant them your peace and your healing.

V. Pray for us, holy Thomas, dear father of the sick:
R. That we may be made worthy of the promises of Christ.

Let us pray:
Eternal Father, in your mercy you granted miracles of grace and healing to all who took shelter in the intercession of your martyr, St Thomas of Canterbury. Through his prayers, look kindly all who suffer, Console them with your presence and in your clemency restore to them health and well being. We ask this through Christ our Lord. Amen.

Prayer for Miracles

Let your power be seen, O Lord God,
and through the prayers of St Thomas Becket
whose fidelity unto death was pleasing in your sight,
grant your graces to all who are in need.
Touch the sick and suffering with your healing hand,
comfort the distressed and dejected,
shed the light of your peace on those in darkness,
grant peace and serenity to troubled hearts.
Draw them in your loving presence, Lord,
and by intercession of St Thomas, your servant,
pour down miracles and graces upon your people.
Amen.

Prayer to St Thomas for Chastity

In time of temptation

I turn to you, blessed Thomas, in my need
and ask your powerful intercession
as I suffer these temptations against purity.
I beg you, dear Saint, to obtain from the Lord
the graces I need to endure:
to be pure in heart, mind and body,
to resist and to pray, to be distracted from sin;
to throw myself onto the mercy of God
and find in his grace freedom from this snare
and strength in my weakness.
Hear my prayer, faithful Thomas,
commend me to our Holy Mother Mary
and to all the Angels, that they may assist me.
Be my champion, O holy martyr and friend,
lead me to Christ in whom I shall find victory.
Amen.

The Excommunications at Vézelay

Prayer for Bishops

Lord God, raise up heroic Shepherds for your people,
Pastors formed in your grace and faithful to the Gospel,
Disciples immersed in the mystery of Christ
and consecrated in the truth of the Faith.
As with your beloved servant, St Thomas of Canterbury,
convert them to your will and make them forgetful of self.
May they be courageous and true,
free of ambition and unfettered by materialism
and their human weakness;
authentic witnesses to hope and generous servants of charity.

May they be true fathers to their people and their priests
and humble sons of the Church.
May they consecrate their hearts and their lives
to the Heart of the Holy Mother of God
that she may form them according to the Heart of her Son.
May they prefer suffering to honour and truth to respectability.
May they rejoice to see their people grow in holiness,
and at the end of their days be counted as faithful servants.

O Lord God, raise up holy Shepherds for your people
as we commend them to the prayers and watchful care
of your holy martyr, their brother, St Thomas of Canterbury.
Amen.

Prayer for Priests

St Thomas, patron of the English clergy
and intercessor for all priests,
pray for our priests
and assist them in all their needs.
Obtain for them from the Lord
the graces they need to fulfil
their vocation as pastors
and preachers of the word.
Remind them of the sacrament they live,
of the manifold graces God will pour over them
through Holy Orders.

Be their refuge, Sweet Martyr of Christ,
in times of difficulty and temptation,
bring them to the Heart of Jesus Christ,
our Eternal High Priest,
so in him they will find strength and peace.
Be their companion when they face loneliness;
and embolden them when they need courage.
Guide them to the faithful celebration of Mass,
and to frequent, fervent prayer
so they may seek and find the fire of Christ's love
and be transformed in its merciful warmth.

O blessed Thomas, watch over our priests,
most especially those who are broken
or in disgrace,
those exhausted by the sacred ministry,
those who have lost fervour and gentleness,
those who no longer believe or are in error.
Be their advocate, St Thomas, and help them,

may the joy you found in the sacred ministry
be theirs to sustain them;
may the power of God which was manifest in you
be manifest also in their lives and ministry.
Amen.

PRAYER FOR COURAGE

St Thomas, in the midst of trials,
you sought the help of God
and received it.
In prayer and in enduring your sufferings,
the Holy Spirit conferred courage upon you
and embracing it, you persevered
to win the crown of martyrdom.
Pray for me that I too may receive
from the Lord the grace of courage
to dispel fear and anxiety
and face the challenges of life.
Like you, may I be strong and sure,
faithful in Christian discipleship
and heroic in striving for virtue.
May I never lose hope,
even when the darkness of this world
surrounds and threatens me,
but confident in the presence
and help of God,
may I surrender myself to Christ
whose light enlightens and defends us.
Stay close to me, St Thomas,
protect me and guide me,
be as a Pillar of Fortitude
to inspire me and lead me
to be fearless and prudent,
joyful and confident in Christ's victory.
Amen.

Eucharistic Prayer to St Thomas

While biographers concentrate on many aspects of St Thomas's life and conversion, few place emphasis on his profound love for the Holy Eucharist and his deeply reverent offering of Holy Mass. During the process of his conversion, his love for the Eucharist increased and it became the source of his strength in his trials and exile.

O holy St Thomas as you found strength,
peace and joy in the Holy Eucharist,
offering Holy Mass with fervent devotion
and often spending time in adoration
before the Eucharistic Jesus,
so now inspire me with a deeper love
for this great Sacrament of Sacraments,
for Jesus truly present in the Sacred Host,
so I too may long for his company
and be nourished by his Body and Blood,
the Banquet of mercy and Salve of souls.
Pray, O blessed priest and bishop,
that I may be drawn into the mystery of Christ
so I may find my true home
in fathomless depths of his love,
and be set alight by the fire of his embrace.
O Jesus, Jesus, Jesus, my beloved Lord,
through the intercession of your Thomas,
have mercy on me, cleanse me of sin,
feed me with your divine life and love,
draw me into your chamber, your Heart
and let me remain there, forever and ever.
Amen.

St Thomas receives a vision of Christ

Prayer in a Time of Need

O St Thomas, I turn to you in my need,
please listen to my prayer,
you who are the Saint of Miracles.
I take refuge in your intercession
and ask that you may now help me
as the commend this my request to you
(mention your petition here).
O blessed Thomas, Solace, Guardian,
Consoler and Friend of Christ our Lord,
be a haven for this poor pilgrim's prayer.
Amen.

Prayer for the Persecuted

Lord Jesus Christ, we commend to you
all who endure persecution;
for your disciples who bear the weight of the cross
for the sake of their faith and love of you.
Through the intercession of your martyr,
St Thomas Becket, who himself bore the yoke
of suffering, alienation and oppression,
grant them peace, patience and strength,
flood their souls with your divine light
so they may, with serenity, endure with hope,
and forgive their oppressors.
May their pains bear fruit for the salvation of souls.
Crown them, Lord Jesus, as your witnesses,
as those most dear to your Heart.

Blessed Thomas, Shield of the Oppressed,
reach down to your suffering brothers and sisters
and assure them of your constant presence
and unfailing prayers. Amen.

Prayer for the Conversion of Souls

Look, St Thomas, to those souls who are lost:
those who have turned away from their God,
those who have lost faith, hope and love,
those who been distracted by error or impurity,
those mastered by ambition or worldly success,
those who, through the trials and labours of life,
have forgotten the loving presence of God;
look to them, sweet Child of Merciful Grace,
be their friend and companion, and gently
draw them back to the loving embrace of Christ.
Amen.

Litany of St Thomas Becket

Lord have mercy on us,
Lord have mercy on us
Christ have mercy on us,
Christ have mercy on us
Lord have mercy on us,
Lord have mercy on us

Christ hear us,
Christ graciously hear us

God the Father of Heaven, *have mercy on us*
God the Son, Redeemer of the world, *have mercy on us*
God the Holy Spirit, *have mercy on us*
Holy Trinity One God, *have mercy on us*

Holy Mary, Mother of God, *pray for us*
Queen of Martyrs

St Thomas of Canterbury, *pray for us*
Faithful Pastor
Valiant Primate
Martyr for Christ
Defender of the Faith
Protector of the Church
Child of Merciful Grace
Hidden Penitent
Zealous Servant of the Holy Spirit
Prey for Justice
Oblation for Peace
Prophet of Liberation
Pillar of Fortitude
Scourge of Tyranny

Shield of the Oppressed
Servant of the Gospel
Advocate of the Poor
Solace of the Deprived
Guardian of the Humble
Consoler of the Distressed
Shelter of the Dejected
Sanctuary of the Hopeless
Father of the Sick
Salve for the Wounded
Restorer of Health
Haven for Pilgrims
Fountain of Miracles
Almoner of Graces
Thaumaturgus of the West
Marvel of the Isles
Heavenly Benefactor
Ark of Intercession
Teacher of Christ's Shepherds
Refuge for Priests
Exemplar for Bishops
Patron of the English clergy
Intercessor for England
Helper of those who invoke you

Lamb of God, Who takes away the sins of the world,
Spare us, O Lord.
Lamb of God, Who takes away the sins of the world,
Graciously hear us, O Lord.
Lamb of God, Who takes away the sins of the world,
Have mercy on us.

Pray for us, O blessed martyr, St. Thomas,
That we may be made worthy of the promises of Christ.

Let us pray:

Grant to us your servants, Almighty Father, through the intercession of your faithful servant and martyr, St Thomas of Canterbury, every grace and blessing, and lead your people on the path of virtue, so that like him they may witness to Christ on earth and attain the heavenly kingdom in the life to come.
Through Christ our Lord. Amen

St Thomas returns from exile

The Seven Stations of St Thomas of Canterbury

(St Thomas Stations)

A Pilgrimage to Canterbury

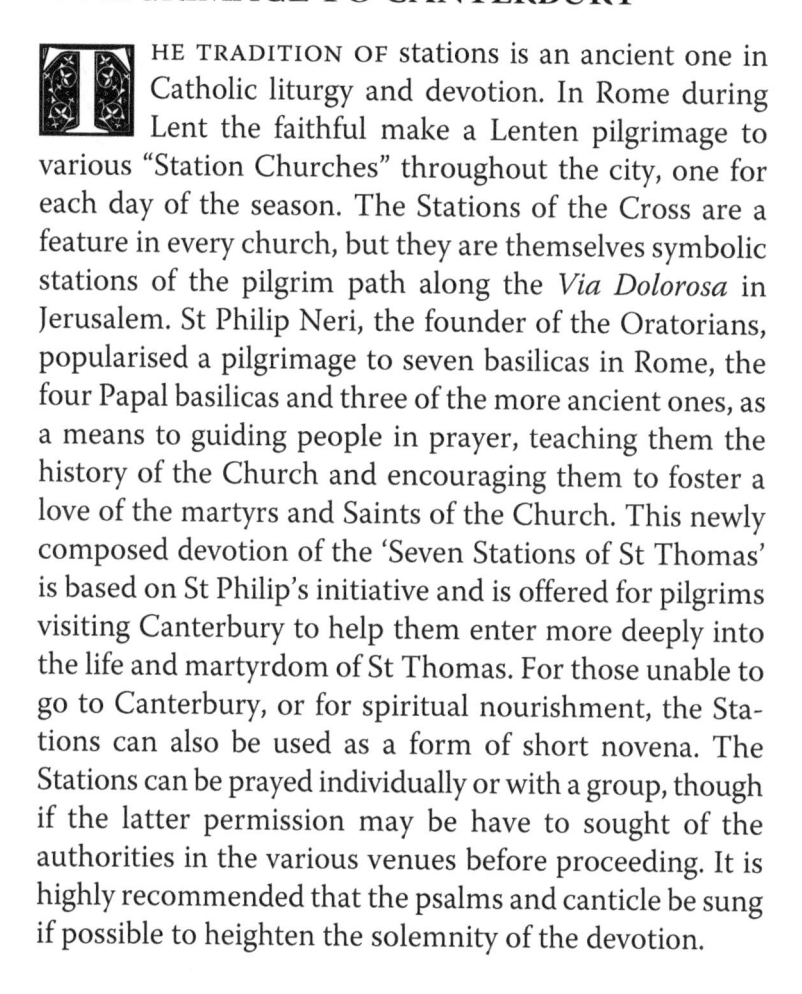

THE TRADITION OF stations is an ancient one in Catholic liturgy and devotion. In Rome during Lent the faithful make a Lenten pilgrimage to various "Station Churches" throughout the city, one for each day of the season. The Stations of the Cross are a feature in every church, but they are themselves symbolic stations of the pilgrim path along the *Via Dolorosa* in Jerusalem. St Philip Neri, the founder of the Oratorians, popularised a pilgrimage to seven basilicas in Rome, the four Papal basilicas and three of the more ancient ones, as a means to guiding people in prayer, teaching them the history of the Church and encouraging them to foster a love of the martyrs and Saints of the Church. This newly composed devotion of the 'Seven Stations of St Thomas' is based on St Philip's initiative and is offered for pilgrims visiting Canterbury to help them enter more deeply into the life and martyrdom of St Thomas. For those unable to go to Canterbury, or for spiritual nourishment, the Stations can also be used as a form of short novena. The Stations can be prayed individually or with a group, though if the latter permission may be have to sought of the authorities in the various venues before proceeding. It is highly recommended that the psalms and canticle be sung if possible to heighten the solemnity of the devotion.

I
ST DUNSTAN'S CHURCH

Built in the 11th Century and dedicated to a former Archbishop of Canterbury, St Dunstan (909–988), it was at this church on the 12 July 1174 that King Henry II began his penitential pilgrimage to the tomb of St Thomas in reparation for his part in the Saint's murder. Divesting himself of his royal regalia, he assumed sackcloth and walked to the cathedral. The church contains the Roper Vault in which the head of St Thomas More rests with the body of his daughter, Margaret Roper. To begin our pilgrimage well, this station is penitential.

O God, come to our aid.
O Lord, make haste to help us.
Glory be to the Father and to the Son and the Holy Spirit. As it was in the beginning, is now and ever shall be, world without end. Amen.

V: Blessed be the Lord our God.
R: In his angels and in his Saints.

Prayer:

Almighty and eternal Father, you sent your Incarnate Son among us to preach the Gospel and to offer his life as a sacrifice for our transgressions, restoring humanity in grace by the gift of mercy. Hear the prayers of your Servant, St Thomas of Canterbury, as we invoke him to plead our cause before you. As you accepted the penances he made in reparation for his sins, pour out the Precious Blood of your Son upon us, forgive us our sins and lead us by the help of your Holy Spirit on the way of salvation. Through Christ our Lord. Amen.

The Miserere: Psalm 50 (51)

Antiphon: In your compassion, hear my cry, O merciful Lord. Renew my heart through the power of your grace.

Have mercy on me, God, in your kindness,
in your compassion blot out my offence.
O wash me more and more from my guilt
and cleanse me from my sin.

My offences truly I know them;
my sin is always before me
Against you, you alone, have I sinned;
what is evil in your sight I have done.

That you may be justified when you give sentence
and be without reproach when you judge,
O see, in guilt I was born,
a sinner was I conceived.

Indeed you love truth in the heart;
then in the secret of my heart teach me wisdom.
O purify me, then I shall be clean;
O wash me, I shall be whiter than snow.

Make me hear rejoicing and gladness,
that the bones you have crushed may thrill.
From my sins turn away your face
and blot out all my guilt.

A pure heart create for me, O God,
put a steadfast spirit within me.
Do not cast me away from your presence,
nor deprive me of your holy spirit.

Give me again the joy of your help;
with a spirit of fervour sustain me,
that I may teach transgressors your ways
and sinners may return to you.

O rescue me, God, my helper,
and my tongue shall ring out your goodness.
O Lord, open my lips
and my mouth shall declare your praise.

For in sacrifice you take no delight,
burnt offering from me you would refuse,
my sacrifice, a contrite spirit,
a humbled, contrite heart you will not spurn.

In your goodness, show favour to Zion:
rebuild the walls of Jerusalem.
Then you will be pleased with lawful sacrifice,
burnt offerings wholly consumed,
then you will be offered young bulls on your altar.
Glory be to the Father and to the Son
and to the Holy Spirit.
As it was in the beginning, is now,
and ever shall be,
world without end. Amen.

Antiphon: In your compassion, hear my cry, O merciful Lord. Renew my heart through the power of your grace.

Reflection:

St Thomas fled to France and was given refuge in the Abbey of St Benedict at Pontigny. There he gave himself to prayer and penance for his sins and his failure to defend Christ, the Church and her people. Fasting, he wore a hairshirt and took the discipline; often spending long nights in vigil before the Lord in the Blessed Sacrament, he beseeched the Lord with fervent prayer: "Lord, be merciful to me a sinner".

V. Though our sins are like scarlet.
R. In your mercy, Lord, you wash us clean again.
V. Praise be the Lord our God.
R. Now and forever! Amen.

Prayer to St Thomas:
O holy St Thomas,
through the action of grace,
God led you from worldly ambition
to become a faithful servant of Christ
and a heroic defender of the Church.
As I struggle with temptation
and the habit of sin,
assist me with your prayers,
that I may open myself
to God's love and strength
and allow him transform me
according to his holy will.
Be my companion, O Blessed Martyr,
counsel me with your wisdom
and intercede for all my needs.
Amen.

Recite the Our Father, a Hail Mary and the Glory be.

St Thomas, penitent of the Lord, *pray for us.*

II
THE PILGRIM WALK

(St Dunstan's Street, St Peter's Street, High Street, Mercery Lane)
In the last days of May 1162, St Thomas made his way along this road to the cathedral to be ordained priest and consecrated bishop. At the end of November 1170 he returned in triumph into his city, his exile over. For centuries pilgrims have walked this street, making their way in piety and often in suffering to the tomb of the martyred archbishop. This station is that of the pilgrim way.

V: Blessed be the Lord our God.
R: In his angels and in his Saints.

Prayer:

Almighty and eternal Father, as we walk the pilgrim path of life in imitation of your Son, Jesus Christ, our Saviour and our Lord, sustain us in all we do, guide us by the work of your Spirit and send your holy servants to accompany us in our daily trials. Through the intercession of your blessed martyr, St Thomas of Canterbury, may we grow in virtue and by your grace, be formed in holiness.
Through Christ our Lord. Amen.

Psalm 120

Antiphon: I will walk in the presence of the Lord in the land of living. And he shall guide my feet on a firm path.

I lift up my eyes to the mountains:
from where shall come my help?
My help shall come from the Lord
who made heaven and earth.

May he never allow you to stumble!
Let him sleep not your guard.
No, he sleeps not nor slumbers,
Israel's guard.

The Lord is your guard and your shade;
at your right hand he stands.
By the day the sun shall not smite you
nor the moon in the night.

The Lord will guard you from evil,
he will guard your soul.
The Lord will guard your going and coming
both now and forever.

Glory be to the Father and to the Son
and to the Holy Spirit.
As it was in the beginning, is now,
and ever shall be,
world without end. Amen.

Antiphon: I will walk in the presence of the Lord in the land of living. And he shall guide my feet on a firm path.

Reflection:

Though it seemed peace had at last been achieved, St Thomas returned to Canterbury rejoicing to see his people again, but also aware that the way to Calvary lay before him. Trusting in the grace of God he was resolved to continue his faithful service of God and the Church, to walk the way of the pilgrim according to the path the will of God decreed. No longer ambitious for the things of this world, he sought the kingdom of heaven and so, at every step, he prayed that he would be made worthy of his office and destiny.

The Holy Rosary is recited.

(Within sight of the cathedral or at the cathedral gate)

Psalm 121

Antiphon: (Alleluia!) Praise God in his Holy Place! In the sanctuary where his holy martyr triumphed.

I rejoiced when I heard them say,
 "Let us go to God's house."
 And now our feet are standing
 within your gates, O Jerusalem.

Jerusalem is built as a city
Strongly compact.
 It is there that the tribes go up,
 the tribes of the Lord.

For Israel's law it is
 There to praise the Lord's name.
 There were set the thrones for judgment,
 of the house of David.

For the peace of Jerusalem pray,
 "Peace be to your homes!
 May peace reign in your walls,
In your palaces, peace!"

For the sake of my brethren and friends,
 I say, "Peace upon you."
 For love of the house of the Lord,
 I will ask for your good.

Glory be to the Father and to the Son
and to the Holy Spirit.
As it was in the beginning, is now,
and ever shall be,
world without end. Amen.

Antiphon: (Alleluia!) Praise God in his Holy Place! In the sanctuary where his holy martyr triumphed.

V. Receive us, O Lord, into your presence.
R. And grant us the joy of the vision of your Face.
V. Praise be the Lord our God.
R. Now and forever! Amen.

Prayer to St Thomas:

St Thomas, true martyr and disciple,
in exile and in suffering
you faithfully walked the pilgrimage of life,
entrusting your needs and fears,
often in the midst of darkness and great danger,
to Christ our Saviour.
Intercede for me,
that I may be resolved to embrace Christ's law
and become a faithful witness
to the Gospel with serenity and hope,
trusting in Christ
and abandoning myself to his providence.
May I come to share your confidence
in Christ's love and fidelity.
Amen.

Recite the Our Father, a Hail Mary and the Glory be.

St Thomas, pilgrim of the Lord, *pray for us.*

III

CANTERBURY CATHEDRAL: CLOISTER

On the day of his martyrdom, 29 December 1170, St Thomas walked this cloister into the north transept to join his monks for Vespers, as he had many times. His killers also took this path to hunt him down. These few yards preserve the saint's last steps on this earth and constitute his physical path to martyrdom.

V: Blessed be the Lord our God.
R: In his angels and in his Saints.

Prayer:

Lord Jesus Christ you tell us, your disciples, to take up our cross and follow you. Through the intercession of your martyred bishop, St Thomas, form us as intentional disciples, embracing our cross in this life and faithfully following you along the path of virtue and holiness, offering whatever suffering we must endure for the glory of your name and the salvation of souls, especially our own. Who lives and reigns forever and ever. Amen.

Psalm 118 (1–20, 24)

Antiphon: 'Take up your cross and follow me', says the Lord.

They are happy whose life is blameless,
who follow God's law!

They are happy those who do his will,
seeking him with all their hearts,
who never do anything evil

but walk in his ways.
You have laid down your precepts
to be obeyed with care.
May my footsteps be firm
to obey your statutes.

Then I shall not be put to shame
as I heed your commands.
I will thank you with an upright heart
as I learn your decrees.
I will obey your statutes:
do not forsake me.

How shall the young remain sinless?
By obeying your word.
I have sought you with all my heart;
let me not stray from your commands.

I treasure your promise in my heart,
lest I sin against you.
Blessed are you, O Lord;
teach me your statutes.

With my tongue have I recounted
the decrees of your lips.
I rejoiced to do your will,
as though all riches were mine.

I will ponder all your precepts,
and consider your paths.
I take delight in your statutes;
I will not forget your word.

Bless your servant and I shall live,

and obey your word.
Open my eyes, that I may consider
the wonders of your law.

I am a pilgrim on the earth;
Show me your commands.
My soul is ever consumed
in longing for your decrees.
Your will is my delight.

Glory be to the Father and to the Son
and to the Holy Spirit.
As it was in the beginning, is now,
and ever shall be,
world without end. Amen.

Antiphon: "Take up your cross and follow me", says the Lord.

Reflection:

In his years as Archbishop, when at the cathedral, Thomas entered into the life of the monks there, praying the Liturgy of the Hours with them when he could. The cloister was a place of peace, but on the last evening of his life it became a battleground, not just with the knights who had come to murder him, but with himself, to trust in God and to expel fear from his heart. This cathedral was a house of prayer, and it was in prayer that Thomas sought refuge and found peace and strength. Prayer helped him carry his cross; it prepared him for his 'crucifixion'

V. Show us, O Lord, the path of holiness.
R. That we may walk in your footsteps.
V. Praise be the Lord our God.

R. Now and forever! Amen.

Prayer to St Thomas:

To you, St Thomas, I entrust my prayer:
that I may humbly take up my cross each day
and faithfully follow our Lord Jesus.
Help me to be forgetful of self,
to put God and neighbour first,
and to joyfully embrace whatever suffering
the Lord sees fit to allow.
Pray, dear saint, that the Lord may guide me
to the wisdom of sacrifice
and to the courage of offering myself
as an oblation to the glory of our God.
Amen.

Recite the Our Father, a Hail Mary and the Glory be.

St Thomas, servant of the will of God, *pray for us*.

The Martyrdom of St Thomas

IV
CANTERBURY CATHEDRAL: "THE MARTYRDOM"

At this spot St Thomas was martyred. The knights struck him down as he prayed and offered his life to Christ for peace, liberty and the protection of the Church. He fell at the altar of St Benedict. His last words: 'For the name of Jesus and the protection of the Church I am ready to embrace death.'

V: Blessed be the Lord our God.
R: In his angels and in his Saints.

Prayer:

Lord Jesus Christ, you who are the joy of the saints and the strength of martyrs, by your death you won for us eternal salvation. Look now upon the death of your servant Thomas, whose blood flowed out for the sake of your name, for peace and freedom. As he united his death to yours, may his intercession be powerful in your sight so with the help of his prayer we may offer our lives as an oblation to your love and endure whatever suffering may come. To you, Lord Jesus, be praise, honour and glory. Amen.

Psalm 21 (12–24)

Antiphon: Take refuge in the Lord, for in him is our life and our joy.

Do not leave me alone in my distress;
come close, there is no one else to help.

Many bulls have surrounded me,
fierce bulls of Bashan close me in.
Against me they open wide their jaws,
like lions, rending and roaring.

Like water I am poured out,
disjointed are all my bones.
My heart has become like wax,
it is melted within my breast.

Parched as burnt clay is my throat,
my tongue cleaves to my jaws.

Many dogs have surrounded me;
a band of the wicked beset me.
They tear holes in my hands and my feet;
and lay me in the dust of death.

I can count every one of my bones.
These people stare at me and gloat;
they divide my clothing among them.
They cast lots for my robe.

O Lord, do not leave me alone,
  my strength, make haste to help me!
Rescue my soul from the sword,
  my life from the grip of these dogs.
Save my life from the jaws of these lions,
  my poor soul from the horns of these oxen.

I will tell of your name to my brethren,
and praise you where they are assembled.
"You who fear the Lord, give him praise;
all sons of Jacob, give him glory.

Revere him, Israel's sons.

Glory be to the Father and to the Son
and to the Holy Spirit.
As it was in the beginning, is now,
and ever shall be,
world without end. Amen.

Antiphon: Take refuge in the Lord, for in him is our life and our joy.

The Martyrdom of St Thomas:

THOMAS STOOD AT his full height and declared that he would defend the Church and her rights and he would not give way, even if they had to kill him. Infuriated the knights threatened him, storming out of the archbishop's chamber. Once outside, the knights went to the mulberry tree to retrieve their swords. Initially Thomas refused to leave his chamber, but ordered his clerks to leave: if he was to die, they would be safe. The monks begged him to come to the cathedral for sanctuary. He refused. In the end, the clerks grabbed hold of him and forcibly took him down to the cloister. Once inside the cathedral, they closed, locked and barricaded the doors, and then begged Thomas to flee; but he refused. Then he said to them 'The Church is a house of prayer and is not to be made into a fortress!' and he ordered the bolt to be drawn back.

Vespers had begun and the choir was chanting the psalms; Thomas began to ascend the steps to choir when the knights barged through the door. They called for the archbishop and Thomas identified himself. The knights demanded the absolution of those Thomas excommunicated; he told them they would be absolved when they repented and made satisfaction. 'Then you will die and receive your just deserts', one of the knights yelled. 'And I am ready to die for my Lord', Thomas responded, 'so that in my blood the Church may obtain peace and liberty.' He continued, 'But I forbid you in the name of God Almighty and on pain of excommunication to harm any of my men, whether clerk or lay.'

The knights rushed at him swords drawn. One urged his companions, 'Strike, strike!' Hearing the words, Thomas knew the time had come and bent forward, covered his eyes with his hands and prayed, 'To God and Mary and the saints who protect and defend this cathedral, and to the blessed St Denis and St Alfege, I commend myself and the Church's cause.' William de Tracy aimed a blow at Thomas's head but cut through his shoulder bone. Edward Grim immediately threw out his arm to protect Thomas taking a blow that almost cut off his arm. Blood was pouring down Thomas's face as he knelt down praying, 'Into thy hands, O Lord, I commend my spirit'.

He stretched out his hands in a gesture to God; de Tracy struck again, slashing at his head causing Thomas to fall at an altar dedicated to St Benedict. 'For the name of Jesus and the protection of the Church', Thomas whispered, 'I am ready to embrace death'. Richard de Britto struck at Thomas's head and sliced off the top of his skull, hitting the flagstones and causing sparks to fly up; the flagstones were shattered with the force. One of the companions to the knights, Hugh of Horsea, came up, put his foot on Thomas's neck and with his sword scraped the brains out of the skull saying, 'This one won't get up again!'

Thomas had been born into eternal life.

V. Precious in the eyes of the Lord.
R. Is the death of his holy one.
V. Praise be the Lord our God.
R. Now and forever! Amen.

Prayer to St Thomas:

May grace and blessing be poured out upon us,
O holy martyr, St Thomas,
as we contemplate your sacrifice
for the sake of Christ and his Church.
Intercede with our Crucified Saviour,
that all who endure persecution for the Faith
may be strengthened by the Holy Spirit
and consoled by the maternal presence
of our most Holy Lady Mary.
May God strengthen them and grant them peace;
may he shield them and grant them wisdom
so they may be faithful to the end
and receive the crown which the Lord
has conferred on you.
Blessed Thomas, pray for them.
Amen.

Recite the Our Father, a Hail Mary and the Glory be.

St Thomas, Martyr for Christ and his Church, *pray for us*.

V
CANTERBURY CATHEDRAL: THE CRYPT

Following his martyrdom, the body of St Thomas was quickly buried in the crypt, the monks fearful that the knights would return to seize the body; like the Lord, he was placed in the tomb almost unwashed and without anointing. This was the first shrine, where the faithful gathered to seek the martyr's intercession until 1220 when a new and greater shrine was constructed in the apse of the cathedral.

V: Blessed be the Lord our God.
R: In his angels and in his Saints.

Prayer:

Heavenly Father, your Son's death and resurrection conquered death and earned for those who faithful to you the promise of resurrection and eternal life. Through the intercession of your servant, Thomas of Canterbury, grant us the grace of enduring faithfully to the end and of placing our trust in you, so you, Lord God, may bring us through the gates of death into your eternal kingdom. Through Christ our Lord. Amen.

Psalm 62 (2–9)

Antiphon: The soul of the just one is in the hands of God, no torment shall ever touch him; he rejoices in the vision of his God.

O God, you are my God; for you I long;
for you my soul is thirsting.
My body pines for you,
like a dry, weary land without water.

So I gaze on you in the sanctuary,
to see your strength and your glory.

For your love is better than life;
my lips will speak your praise.
I will bless you all my life;
in your name I will lift up my hands.
My soul shall be filled as with a banquet;
my mouth shall praise you with joy.

On my bed I remember you.
On you I muse through the night,
for you have been my help;
in the shadow of your wings I rejoice.
My soul clings to you;
your right hand holds me fast.

Glory be to the Father and to the Son
and to the Holy Spirit.
As it was in the beginning, is now,
and ever shall be,
world without end. Amen.

Antiphon: The soul of the just one is in the hands of God, no torment shall ever touch him; he rejoices in the vision of his God.

Reflection:

Thomas's pilgrimage ended and he was laid to rest in this crypt. Fearful that the knights would return to take the body, the monks quickly removed his vestments to discover a monk's habit and then under that a hairshirt, revealing the Archbishop's life of consecration and penance. Like the Lord, they had no time to wash him properly or anoint his body. They dressed him in the vestments he wore at his episcopal consecration, placing his chalice, ring, gloves, sandals and his crozier upon his body. They then buried him weeping, for they loved him. When he first came to them they thought him a creature of the king, but in his struggle for truth and freedom, and with his growth in holiness, he became their father.

V. They shall rest in peace from all their labours.
R. Those whose lives were pleasing to the Lord.
V. Praise be the Lord our God.
R. Now and forever! Amen.

Prayer to St Thomas:

O blessed Thomas, hear my prayer,
and most kindly remember
those who have gone before us
marked with the sign of faith,
and those who mourn their passing.
Today I commend to your intercession
(remember individuals who have died).
Pray that all Christians may be filled
with the hope of Christ's resurrection,
and that we may be mindful
of the souls in Purgatory.
Help us to live our lives as pilgrims,
serving Christ and the Gospel on earth
with our hearts and hopes
set on the Kingdom of Heaven.
Amen.

Recite the Our Father, a Hail Mary and the Glory be.

St Thomas, victorious in death, *pray for us.*

The Shrine of St Thomas

VI
CANTERBURY CATHEDRAL: THE SITE OF THE TOMB

From 1220 to the shrine's destruction in 1538 this was the site of St Thomas tomb, the goal of the pilgrimage of countless men and women from all over England and Europe. Here they poured out their hearts to St Thomas, here the sick came seeking healing, here distraught clergy sought peace, here the Church reflected and marveled at his life and death and at his continual concern for the children of God.

V: Blessed be the Lord our God.
R: In his angels and in his Saints.

Prayer:

Almighty Father, through the gracious intercession of your martyr, St Thomas of Canterbury, hear the fervent prayers of your people. On the sick, pour out the graces of your healing; on the distressed, your peace; the lost, your guidance; the doubtful, the gift of faith; on your Church, unity; and all on who invoke you your manifold blessings. May your people always rejoice in your presence and in the loving friendship of your servant Thomas. Through Christ our Lord. Amen.

Psalm 150

Strophe:
O blessed Thomas, rejoice in the heavenly kingdom,
for now you see the Lord our God as he really is.
O blessed Thomas, pray for us, poor pilgrims,
that one day we too may share in your delights.

Alleluia!

Praise God in his holy place;
praise him in his mighty heavens.
Praise him for his powerful deeds;
praise his surpassing greatness.

Strophe:
O blessed Thomas, rejoice in the heavenly kingdom,
for now you see the Lord our God as he really is.
O blessed Thomas, pray for us, poor pilgrims,
that one day we too may share in your delights.

O praise him with sound of trumpet;
praise him with lute and harp.
Praise him with timbrel and dance,
praise him with strings and pipes.

Strophe:
O blessed Thomas, rejoice in the heavenly kingdom,
for now you see the Lord our God as he really is.
O blessed Thomas, pray for us, poor pilgrims,
that one day we too may share in your delights.

O praise him with resounding cymbals;
praise him with clashing of cymbals.
Let everything that lives and that breathes
give praise to the Lord!

Alleluia!

Strophe:
O blessed Thomas, rejoice in the heavenly kingdom,
for now you see the Lord our God as he really is.

O blessed Thomas, pray for us, poor pilgrims,
that one day we too may share in your delights.

Glory be to the Father and to the Son
and to the Holy Spirit.
As it was in the beginning, is now,
and ever shall be,
world without end. Amen.

Strophe:
O blessed Thomas, rejoice in the heavenly kingdom,
for now you see the Lord our God as he really is.
O blessed Thomas, pray for us, poor pilgrims,
that one day we too may share in your delights.

Reflection:

Just moments after his martyrdom, people in the cathedral for Vespers came to the martyr's body to venerate it and take relics. The blood that was shed was brought to the sick and dying and many recovered. A torrent of miracles poured out upon Canterbury, upon England and throughout the Church. The Lord had accepted his bishop's sacrifice and now it was to bear fruit: in the vision of God for his servant and in a multitude of graces falling from heaven upon earth at his intercession. None of those who came to the great Ark in which St Thomas's body was laid was forgotten; he heard their prayers and in the sight of God he raised his arms in supplication. And Thomas prays: "Lord God, you are my God, hear my prayer: pour out your grace upon your people".

V. May the wonders of the Lord be manifest.
R. In the lives of his faithful people.
V. Praise be the Lord our God.

R. Now and forever! Amen.

Prayer to St Thomas:

O holy martyr, St Thomas,
O great intercessor, Fountain of miracles,
hear the prayers of all who invoke you.
Receive into the mantle of your fatherly care
the sick and the distressed,
those burdened by the trials of life,
those who have lost hope, the fearful
and all who are in need.
Keep watch over our priests and bishops,
sustain them in their lives and ministry
and obtain for them the graces they need
to be faithful, loving and strong.
Intercede, sweet Thomas, for this my request
(mention your intention here).
Amen.

Recite the Our Father, a Hail Mary and the Glory be.

St Thomas, intercessor for the children of God, *pray for us.*

St Thomas enters Paradise

VII
PARISH CHURCH OF ST THOMAS OF CANTERBURY: MARTYRS' CHAPEL

This parish church, dedicated to St Thomas, is now the Catholic shrine of the martyr. Relics of the saint are preserved in the Chapel of Martyrs and constitute the few relics that now remain: at the beginning of English Reformation his body was quickly buried in an unknown location by monks to escape the destruction of the shrine as ordered by Henry VIII. These few physical remains serve to remind the Church of Thomas's continual presence and intercession.

V: Blessed be the Lord our God.
R: In his angels and in his Saints.

Prayer:

Let us rejoice in your presence, Lord God, and forever proclaim your mighty works. May the life, death and glorious intercession of your martyr and bishop, St Thomas of Canterbury, inspire your people to seek holiness and, filled with joy, be ardent witnesses to the Gospel and your work for the salvation of all souls. We ask this through Christ our Lord. Amen.

Canticle: (Cf. Revelation 19:5, 6–8)

Antiphon: Let us sing a canticle of praise to God, for he has raised up in our midst our beloved brother Thomas, offered as an oblation to Christ.

Praise our God, you servants of his,

and all who, great and small, revere him.
Alleluia!
The reign of the Lord our God Almighty has begun;
let us be glad and joyful and give praise to God,
because this is the time for the marriage of the Lamb.

His bride is ready,
and she has been able to dress herself in dazzling white linen,
because her linen is made of the good deeds of the saints.

Happy are those who are invited
to the wedding feast of the Lamb.

Glory be to the Father and to the Son
and to the Holy Spirit.
As it was in the beginning, is now,
and ever shall be,
world without end. Amen.

Antiphon: Let us sing a canticle of praise to God, for he has raised up in our midst our beloved brother Thomas, offered as an oblation to Christ.

From the Letters of St Thomas Becket: (From *Epistle 74*)

Remember, then, how our fathers were saved; how the Church has grown, and with what sufferings she has increased. Remember the storms the ship of Peter has weathered, with Christ as passenger. Remember how they have attained a crown, whose faith has come to shine more brightly through tribulation. So it is that the throng of the saints has grown. The saying remains true for all time, "Only he who has fought the good fight receives the crown."

Beatus Vir

(Ps 1:1–3; Ps 2: 7b–12; Ps 115:15; Ps 111:1; Ps 112: 1b–2)

Blessed indeed is the man
who follows not the counsel of the wicked;
nor lingers in the way of sinners
nor sits in the company of scorners,
but whose delight is the law of the Lord
and who ponders his law day and night.

He is like a tree that is planted
beside the flowing waters,
that yields its fruit in due season
and whose leaves shall never fade;
and all that he does shall prosper.

The Lord said to me: "You are my son.
It is I who have begotten you this day.
Ask and I shall bequeath you the nations,
put the ends of the earth in your possession.
With a rod of iron you will break them,
shatter them like a potter's jar.

Now, O kings, understand,
take warning rulers of the earth;
serve the Lord with awe
and trembling, pay him your homage
lest he be angry and you perish;
for suddenly his anger will blaze.

Blessed are they who put their trust in God.
O precious in the eyes of the Lord
is the death of his faithful.

O blessed is the man who fears the Lord,
who takes delight in his commands.

Praise, O servants of the Lord,
praise the name of the Lord!
May the name of the Lord be blessed
both now and forever more!

Glory be to the Father and to the Son
and to the Holy Spirit.
As it was in the beginning, is now,
and ever shall be,
world without end. Amen.

Intercessions:

(The following intercessions or similar may now be offered)

Lord God, through the intercession of your martyr, St Thomas, hear our prayers for your Church and for the world.

Defend the Church against all dangers and sustain her in her trials; grant her unity and peace.
Lord hear our prayer.

Protect N. our Pope, N. our Bishop, and all bishops, priests and deacons; may they be faithful as St Thomas was faithful.
Lord hear our prayer.

Watch over our missionaries and assist them in their work of proclaiming the Gospel.
Lord hear our prayer.

Grant your strength to all Christians who are suffering for their faith.
Lord hear our prayer.

Inspire men and women to heed your call to offer their lives in service to the Gospel and the Church.
Lord hear our prayer.

Preserve the world in peace and guide those who govern us.
Lord hear our prayer.

Pour out your grace upon the sick, the distressed, the poor, the afflicted and all in need.
Lord hear our prayer.

Grant your blessing to married couples and their children, deepen their love and help them.
Lord hear our prayer.

Grant to the faithful departed eternal rest and the vision of your Face.
Lord hear our prayer.

V. May the Lord hear the prayers of his servants.
R. And bless his people with peace.
V. Praise be the Lord our God.
R. Now and forever! Amen.

Prayer to St Thomas:

O you, Blessed Thomas,
I commend my prayers and my life,
watch over me and protect me.

O holy martyr and Primate,
faithful servant of Christ and valiant disciple,
may I too seek to serve my Lord
and to love him above all others,
with all my heart, mind, will and strength;
that my life may be a praise of glory to his Name.
Assist me in this endeavour, dear Thomas,
so my life may be pleasing to him
and of service to his holy Church.
With you, dear Saint, I pray:
May the Lord be blessed and praised
forever and ever!
Amen.

Recite the Our Father, a Hail Mary and the Glory be.

St Thomas, crowned in glory, *pray for us.*

Let us pray:

Almighty and eternal Father,
may this votive commemoration of the life and sufferings of your servant, St Thomas of Canterbury,
obtain for us, through the intercession of your blessed Martyr,
every grace and blessing,
that we may attain holiness of life and your help in all our trials.
Through our Lord Jesus Christ who lives and reigns with you
in the unity of the Holy Spirit, one God, forever and ever.
Amen.

Salve Regina

Salve, Regina, mater misericordiae;
vita, dulcedo et spes nostra, salve.
Ad te clamamus exsules filii Hevae.
Ad te suspiramus gementes et flentes
in hac lacrimarum valle.
Eia ergo, advocata nostra,
illos tuos misericordes oculos ad nos converte.
Et Iesum, benedictum fructum ventris tui,
nobis post hoc exsilium ostende.
O clemens, o pia, o dulcis Virgo Maria.

Lightning Source UK Ltd.
Milton Keynes UK
UKHW040602291118
333139UK00001B/15/P

9 780852 449141